The View from the Villa Delirium

Brian Docherty

The View from the Villa Delirium
© Brian Docherty
First Edition 2021

Cover image: 'In the Hills' by Kate Gritton

Published under Dempsey & Windle's VOLE imprint

Dempsey & Windle
15 Rosetrees
Guildford
Surrey
GU1 2HS
UK
01483 571164
dempseyandwindle.com

British Library Cataloguing-in-Publication Data
A catalogue record for this book is available from the British
Library
ISBN: 978-1-913329-51-8

Printed in the UK by Imprint Digital (Exeter)

By the same author

Armchair Theatre
A Desk with A View
Woke Up This Morning
Independence Day
In My Dreams, Again
Only In St. Leonards: A Year On The Marina
Blue to the Edge

Acknowledgements

Acknowledgements are due to the following magazines, anthologies, and websites:

Acumen; Brittle Star, *di-vêrsé-city 2021*: the annual anthology of Austin International Poetry Festival; *Dream Catcher*; *FED Writing Challenge*; *Hastings Independent*; *Hastings Online Times*; *Live Canon 2017 Anthology; London Grip; Mistress Quickly's Bed*; *Places of Poetry*: placesofpoetry.org.uk; *Poetry Space Showcase*; YourPoemaDay.

'Junkyard Squirrel' was awarded the Josephine Austin Silver Cup for Poetry, 2018.

Again, to my Secret Sisterhood

Contents

GOOD BREAD

A man walks out of a wet Monday into a Baker's,
queues, says to the woman behind the counter,
'Have you got a small sesame seed bloomer?'
because that is what he wants most in the world
at that moment, but she looks at him, gestures
behind her, 'No, we've sold out, but I have got . . .'

He buys another loaf, not quite what he wanted,
but a loaf nevertheless, looks at the woman,
who is grey-eyed, dark-haired, beautiful,
who would light up the town if she smiled,
and recalls someone he knew in a previous life,
then brings himself back to this present moment.

'Could you save me one tomorrow please?'
She bestows a smile, 'I don't know, we're busy
here, maybe . . .' he nods, looks her in the eye,
'You're a baker, you know what good bread means.'
She says 'Yes' as if she knows what he is thinking,
A loaf of bread, a jug of wine, a book of verse, and thou.

Would she quote the *Rubiáyát* of Omar Khayyám
that she learnt by heart as a child here, or wherever
she grew up, maybe she is also a poet or musician,
plays in pubs & wine bars from here to Brighton,
but this bakery provides her daily bread in every sense,
she knows how much her bread means to her customers.

But when she closes the shop door on her working day,
that door stays closed, she forgets that part of her life
for a few hours, but the man cannot know that,
thinks only of the loaf in his hand and her smile,
is warmed by that, will go to the florist for daffodils,
walk home happier, and enjoy his lunch with Radio 3.

THE SMALLEST THING

Can be a woman's secret smile,
made of some of the atoms that make
her who she is, and you look at her,
look away, and she is still smiling,
now you think *Could this be a lucky
day,* or is she remembering the feeling
of sand between her toes, or a lawn
walked over to greet a special friend,
and you want to catch her eye, move
towards her and see what happens next.

Maybe something, maybe nothing,
and you are glad she has something
to smile about and brighten her day
but now you don't want to intrude on
her personal space, but how good
it would feel if that smile could be
for you, and maybe you could talk
together then, even for a moment,
and you wonder if you are channelling
Roy Orbison, and hold yourself still.

Maybe she won't remember this moment
at all, but you will think of the way that
smile made her a lamp, lit from within
for herself, and for anyone lucky enough
to be part of her life, and you walk on,
and oh yes, her eyes were the purest
cornflower blue, and of course her
hair complemented them perfectly
and if you thought about absent friends,
well, you can do that now and smile.

THE STAR IN YOUR HEART
(after Dawn Timmins, *To The Stars*)

Is that really where this couple are going?
They are the classic couple, the sailor
and his lass, his retro chic striped jersey
and her green hair could pass unnoticed
in Brighton, or even Hastings nowadays,
and the big red heart they share would
have all their friends singing Bob Marley,
'One love, one heart' until they realise
she really is a mermaid, and she is far out
of her element, yet pulling him onwards.

And yes, they are headed for the stars now,
they are stars in their own private world,
upwards, ever upwards, till they reach orbit
or escape velocity, she is older than he can
possibly know, but he will lend his energy
gladly, and the stars shine brighter, getting
closer, the sea and the boat below receding
but still visible till they are out of atmosphere,
and only true love will power them now,
and there can be no doubts or second thoughts.

And still the stars shine on, as they mostly
always have done, perhaps one has gone
supernova, and we down below will not notice
for lightyears to come, but our young couple
will take their place united as one new star
to shine on, and shine down on us, and if
their friends ever think *What happened to them*,
they have only to look up, or into their hearts,
and know that on the darkest night, there
is always one star that will shine for them.

SLOW DATING
(after Dawn Timmins, *Coffee and Cake*)

Mermaids' perfect and beautiful power
means they have no need to make deals
with the mundane world; they take what
they want, on their terms, ignore the rest.

So here she is on the rocks at low tide,
entertaining her latest young man.
There have been so many, she thinks
he is Tom, turns them all into Toms.

Tom thinks he is here for tea & cake,
possibly imagines he is in a café on
St. Leonards seafront, maybe *Kassa*,
but she knows exactly where they are.

She has done this after the new moon
for 400 years, they all merged into
the same man long ago, but the 4pm
ritual remains unchanged and perfect.

All Tom knows is that she is green
and silver and beautiful, he would
take off his clothes and run into
the sea if that is what she desires.

She might, or she could make herself
invisible to him, leave a sliver of pain
in his heart, leave him looking with
longing at every woman with green hair.

BLUE DAY
(after Dawn Timmins, *Picnic Basket*)

Today, she is blue, but might be green
again tomorrow, depending on what
happens later today, and how far into
the Sussex countryside he takes her.

This mermaid, in all her long life,
has never been so far from shore,
has never been on a red bicycle,
but knows what a red light means.

She likes the man's red beard, his blue
striped jersey, his blue woollen hat,
his laugh, but he is only a man after all,
who has no idea what her basket holds.

He only had eyes for the bottle of Vin,
never read the rest of the label, or asked
what food it might accompany, maybe
thinking bread, cheese, pâté, and grapes.

Soon, he will find a spot on the Downs
with a sea view, he will kneel to her,
take her hand and offer her his heart,
then she will give him red, red, wine.

She will stop his mouth with seaweed
soaked in wine, and take his little heart.
He will return her to Rock-a-Nore, recall
nothing later, but she will be green again.

MARIANNE
(after Dawn Timmins, *Mermaid on a Motorbike*)

She is gracing the bike's pillion seat,
playing Marianne Faithfull for the day
at the earnest request of her steersman,
who baffled her with talk of some movie.

She does not understand monochrome,
his black leather, helmet, black bike,
or why he is so proud of this Vincent
Black Shadow, why her hair is black.

She is green and silver, and proud of it,
shining handmaiden to Stella Maris,
and is given leave to go ashore today
to attend the March of the Mermaids.

She, and some *Special Guest* sisters,
will blend in with Brighton women,
drink pale ale & rum in the pub later,
and show them how to dance a polka.

Anything else that happens, whatever
secrets are shared, are their business,
this Dave she glamoured at low tide
can live his life happily in 1968.

Perhaps his brain froze at puberty,
she has given up on men, sail or shore;
as long as he returns her to Rock-a-Nore
before moonrise, she can tolerate him.

DANCING THE HARVEST IN
(after Keith Tyson, *Under A Harvest Moon He Works 24 Hours A Day*)

I'm still not sure what happened in that field
or whether I dreamt it while lying in a ditch

on the way home from *The Stag*; my good wife
says she left me talking to some Morris dancers,

went home to watch a *Midsomer Murders* repeat,
found me seated at the kitchen table gone 4 am.

I was wet, cold, muddy, but otherwise unharmed,
apart from this green rune gracing my forehead.

Was that personage under the full moon a demon,
a Green Man gone feral, or a local prank aimed at

outlandish folks like me? Whoever or whatever,
he danced across the field, out and back, round

and round, his naked feet crunched the stubble,
curled up and pointed like mediaeval shoes, moving

to a music only he could hear, red mouth leering,
long pitchfork miming a sea sprite's trident, is he

the mermaids' cousin, and what was in his left hand?
Under that moon, it could have been a bat, a bottle,

or something mortal folk do not need to know about,
only be thankful it is not aimed at them in earnest.

As for his work, as long as the beer and bread are good,
my friends will welcome his avatar at Jack in the Green.

HOW FAR IS TOO FAR?
(after Adrienne Hunter, *We Went Further Than We Intended*)

As if you could reach Too Far, but we did go there,
along a narrowing path till the cliff baffled us.

No way up, down or round, a crumble underfoot,
a slip of scree that promised a dance downhill

we would not forget if survived, we are too old
for temptation, learnt to stop at *not quite enough*,

to resist *one for the road*, or take the last train.
Getting back, from There to Here, is never boring,

we leave those adventures to our grandchildren,
we stained the t-shirt, got our money's worth

from the NHS, in bandages, crutches, scars,
and a box of memories we prefer not to open.

So call us cautious, our motto *this far and no farther*,
our goal home in time for dinner & wine with friends.

So we gather, raise a glass to absent or scattered friends,
there is always an empty or extra chair for anyone new

or old pals who text from Gatwick, **What's in the pot,
save some, you wouldn't believe where I've been.**

But we will, as long as you're here in person, Facebook
is a parallel universe to us, we enjoy those glimpses,

but we like our friends Here, while we are still here,
and our table is not too far and the wine within reach.

VANISHING BEACH
(after Adrienne Hunter, *We Lost Track of Time*)

Perhaps we strolled the strand too slowly
skirting the loose scree at the cliff bottom.

Yes, we read the signs, looked up and said
'We'll hear it and just run or jump aside.'

We assumed the tide would have come in early
for the fishermen, didn't read the tide tables.

So when we noticed the beach was shrinking
we said 'Oh, look' and carried on searching

for a way up to Cliff End village; we nearly got
a way up to Heaven, almost out of sight of help,

then our path narrowed to a swirl sweeping away
our plans, hiding the rocks we had walked past,

now we had to run ankle-deep, then knee-deep,
the last bit of beach almost too far, slip, soak,

scrape, knee bang, too wet and breathless
to shout at each other; we did that later.

We didn't even stop at any of the pubs or cafes,
no taxi's, a long cold walk, no excuses, one slap.

You don't need to know the promises made,
how those moments changed our lives.

We are still here, but something was lost,
for the next week our friends didn't dare ask.

A VIEW OF HASTINGS CASTLE
(after Jennifer Baird, *Autumn Sunset Over Hastings Castle*)

In this view, the Castle mimes Glastonbury Tor,
taking us back to a time when the Somerset Levels
were under water, and we needed a raft or coracle
to get about, and the Tor was our holy island.

A place of magic where people gathered,
met cousins, and strangers who became friends,
their lives infused by the energies from the Tor,
and the great circle of bluestones down below.

We don't need to believe in ley lines to know
that we have come to Hastings for a new life,
we can stand on the West Hill and look down
on the Stade where Duke William didn't land.

We have no fear of men with swords now,
but the Castle still watches over us, our local
Folly, reminding us we are a seaside town,
the sea may feed us, but is never our friend.

No battle was ever fought over this Castle,
but the sea took parts whenever it wanted,
not enough left to construct a Gothic ruin,
nor dramatic enough for a scene in *Foyle's War*.

Nothing happens in our Castle, we like it
that way, our local mantra is *In Hastings
we do things different*; if you want some
truth about this Castle, write it yourself.

VIEW FROM THE JERWOOD GALLERY
(after David Reeve, *The Stade*)

Welcome to our Invisible Harbour,
this moveable feast is typical Hastings,
even the famous battle didn't happen here,
Duke William wouldn't risk his longships.

This Gallery stole part of our strand,
I came here once, liked the art, the cafe,
couldn't enjoy the view; now art lovers
come and look down on us, *how picturesque.*

We are fisherfolk still, luggers drawn up
by tractors now, my grandfather recalled
horses and capstans, gone like the fish he knew,
the Old Town too posh now for the likes of us.

But as long as there are tides and stars,
and black huts to dry our nets, we will work
while you sleep, we are not an Art Installation
or Heritage Museum, so come buy our fish.

Don't even think about a Yachting Marina,
we like this beach, what's left, as is, untidy,
traces of our working life everywhere,
and no, we don't offer Day Trips to Margate.

So put your iDevice away, just look for once,
remember the colours, the boat numbers,
think about why we are registered in Rye,
why we wouldn't have it any other way.

LUGGER
(after David Reeve, *Abandoned Boat, Dungeness*)

We are abandoned here, but not desolate.
Some of us chose to settle by the sea,
others were washed up or stranded here,
came for a day or weekend, just never left.

Maybe that's what happens in every desert
from Gobi to Sonora, people drawn there
by inherited memory of a phantom sea,
but we pilgrims are called to the real thing.

Perhaps some ancestor crewed a lugger,
Galway hooker, dhow, or Viking longship,
and here they are, friends and neighbours,
each with a story taller than a tea clipper.

We love our desert, tolerate Dungeness B,
don't mind the tourists or Derek Jarman fans
who ask us if we knew him, or were extras
in his films, and we never disappoint them.

If we tell them this lugger was Mr Jarman's,
to catch his dinner menu with his own hands,
and he gathered samphire and dulse as garnish,
why would they not take our script as gospel?

And if one of us says 'I was his boy ashore',
they can make of that what they will, we won't
say he worked the winch, we are local colour,
salty dogs, enacting a thousand years of history.

HALF-LIFE
(after David Reeve, *Abandoned Huts, Dungeness*)

Everything here is abandoned, even Dungeness A
Power Station, but the residual energy lives on.

And England's only desert will live on
while the rest of Kent, Sussex, & Suffolk

and who knows what else, crumbles away
and any memories the soil & chalk hold

go to feed the fishes, or amuse the mermaids;
they won't tell what went on in these huts,

people's little lives, the pitiful half-life
of human hearts fading away so soon.

What happens on shore stays on shore
might be one way they look at our world

until we venture out to sea, or walk by
their rocks under the new moon, and then

they may take an interest, might even let
the Selkies come ashore in their other guise.

But even they if could, the mermaids would not
come near these huts, they feel the black energy

in their hearts, on their skin, know the big grey
block running its heavy water into their water

could mean the end of everything, an abandoned
world, with no berth for them on the last starship.

EVERYTHING FALLS APART
(after Amanda Averillo, *At Dungeness*)

But this is not a wasteland, our ecology
is mutable but not yet mutant; who knows
what our dark neighbour could visit on us.

If anyone who might know cares to drop by
for more than 30 seconds without suiting up,
we will offer a traditional Kentish welcome.

Meanwhile, we will salvage, reclaim, recycle
everything still standing. We have read Margaret
Mead, are your native cargo cult, donate Here.

Perhaps part of this hut, these boats, will turn up
in an Art Gallery near you as sculpture or frames,
or as furniture in the North Laine or St. Leonards.

What's left might grace our cottages as Found Art,
when we're bored we burn it on cold winter nights,
or our kids use it for bonfires, and smoke seaweed.

Whatever we do with the wreckage of our former lives
is our business, we live in the Now, can't afford nostalgia,
we might take the money and costumes as a Derek Jarman

Theme Park, or Heritage Lottery Fund Visitor Experience,
if that is ever a post-Brexit possibility, or Independence
for Kent comes next; the tide comes in, the tide goes out.

But today, buy us a drink, no selfies, catch the last bus
to Roseland, we ain't your cabaret, try the Copper Family
over Brighton way for that, and don't upset the mermaids.

A PLACE OF SAFETY
(after Cathy Bird, *Fairfield Church*)

Where may sheep safely graze? If not
here on Romney Marsh, by the red roof
of Thomas à Becket Church, then where?

The grazing is good, the sheep are fat,
they are content to live in their Now,
only one one predator to worry them.

Four of those defiled Canterbury Cathedral,
disgraced their knightly vows during Vespers
and took the life and light of that holy man.

And where was the Good Shepherd that day,
or was calling Becket away from his flock
another part of a Plan we cannot understand?

These sheep will be called to the knife one day,
and even if they know this church roof is red,
they live in blue and green, stoic to their end.

But today the sky is blue, the grass is sweet,
there are no people or dogs in sight or sound,
and for once, no new colours to frighten them.

This square of salt marsh, with the church
they have no need to enter, is their only home,
and they are as safe here as anywhere.

Tomorrow might be different, they might swim
to safety while the butcher sleeps, or we might
all turn vegan overnight, and let them alone.

We are all beasts in the eyes of The Lord,
and if this life on this planet is a Theatre,
let us be better next time by acting with love.

READING VAN GOGH

With or without his letters to Theo,
takes us somewhere we may not
wish to go, wondering how Vincent
got there, distracted by Gauguin,
tormented by the girl he followed
from Paris to Arles, only to discover
she was oblivious to this strangest
of men, and unable to ease his
unrequited love, not knowing
what to do with his severed ear.

If only he had brought flowers,
shop bought, or the sunflowers
he painted out in those July fields,
she might have responded with
kindness or indifference, or said
'Oh m'sieur, they are lovely,
but I already have an admirer.'
Or he could have sketched her,
and she hid it away in an attic or
put it in a drawer, until one day,

when she had almost forgotten him,
she might learn of his genius,
and say 'Oh, I knew him when
I was nineteen, and he and the
other lunatic painted and drank,
drank again, then painted on,
nobody understanding what
they were doing, and you know
what, he gave me something
one evening, what is it worth?'

THE HAPPY PLACE

Is your very own seat of choice
in the library you like best, on a
summer's day, when everyone else
is in the park or on the beach or
sitting outside the pub under an
umbrella with a pint, or a pitcher
of Pimm's, and they think there is
nowhere else they would rather be,
without a care in the world, and
would if they thought about it,

pity you, indoors on a day like
today, but it is you who are truly
happy to have this cool, quiet,
space almost to yourself, able to
read anything you choose for a
minute or an hour, and maybe
finger your way along the desire
paths of shelves you rarely visit,
perhaps even a section of the library
you have never explored properly,

shyly opening books on subjects
you have never been interested in
before, and might never be again,
so you will make the most of today,
because tomorrow your best friend
might say 'Let's go to the beach'
or 'Have you ever been to Knole'
and you will go gladly because
you only want to make them happy,
and today might remain your secret.

NEW LIFE, NEW LOVE

(after Jess Norgrove, *She Lives In A Fairytale*)

This is genuine Gothic, not Strawberry Hill's
papier-mâché confection, but good local stone,
could be anywhere, Tintagel to Transylvania,
not a fantasy, but as real as anything can be.

Her sky or the ruined ceiling mirroring it,
is blue, but the stars have fallen to the floor,
lost in the rubble, maybe ground underfoot,
any crystal, windows or goblets, long gone.

Even the staircase, to be ascended or descended
at will, to the grand ballroom or reception room,
is eroded, usable at your own risk, in daylight.
Our heroine is indifferent but not oblivious.

Electricity, hot water, central heating, are not
her concern, are someone else's fantasy for this
house, she has managed for four hundred years,
and will never look a day older than twenty-two.

She has never thought of dying, or growing up,
has never heard blues or jazz, has never been
to a concert or art gallery, she has no interest
in princes or slippers, no wicked step-mother.

She knows her Princess will come to save her,
will give her the new world and new life
she deserves, and that this will be more real
than any fantasy, and she will know true love.

GREETINGS FROM TORBAY

The first thing I notice here is seaweed,
that familiar tang from childhood holidays,
and I want laver to purée into laverbread,
to spice up my GP's Five A Day Challenge.

I'd like to find the dulse and sea purslane
shown in *Edible Seaweeds of the World,*
or some tansy or samphire from the cliffs
above the bay; I am too cautious to climb.

I'll take a bag of weed home for Maria,
a token of esteem, but not books or jewellery,
her cue to smile and say 'You're bonkers.'
I hope she'll gift me bounty from her garden.

I want my five a day from Maria's garden,
her courgettes were gorgeous, I want more,
I want her potatoes, tomatoes, kale, carrots,
her sweet peas, whatever Maria offers up.

But if she chooses to give her good things
to her Brighton girlfriends, or someone new,
the mermaids will whisper *Big boys don't cry,*
remind me Maria might walk a different path.

Will Maria admit my seaweed to her kitchen,
fry it, steam it, make it a side dish if she can't
trust it, post the results on Facebook, slap me
if it ruins her pan, or feed it to the badgers?

WITH A LITTLE HELP

I thought life was improving till Hogmanay,
and my dear friend announced her house was on
the market and she was moving back to Planet B.

I was watching Jools Holland's *Hootenanny,*
comfortably numb till I heard Jose Feliciano
& Jools Holland perform 'As you see me now'.

A glass of port and a bottle of Old Crafty Hen
will do that for you, I even sang 'Auld Lang Syne'
after the Bells, watching the pipers strut their stuff.

Today the mermaids did call & response to Joe Cocker's
version of 'With a Little Help from My Friends',
and yes, friends, I am seeking someone to love.

Then in Alexandra Park doing walking meditation,
I heard traffic going from Here to There & Back,
geese, flowing water, dog lovers sniffing each other.

In this grey light the landscape is more blurred than
a Monet, green merges into russet; I am not weeping,
I am not lost, soon I will be on my way home.

An empty flat full of things from a previous life,
our lives change, but if shared paths diverge,
who needs Virtual Reality when we have Facebook.

So we go on, friends for life, only 10 parsecs apart,
my craft can reach her parallel universe any time,
till the day she says 'What are you doing here?'

'I was looking for a friend' could be my last word,
or the first thing I say in the next pub I walk into,
to the first man, woman or Other who says 'Hello.'

SNOW PAUSES SUSSEX

I am just going outside and may be some time. (Captain Oates)

If I were an officer and a gentleman,
I might consider making that sacrifice,
this morning I am intent on staying alive,
my boiler works, no danger of hypothermia.

I shall not slip in the bath, but do need
to trudge out for bread and lunch, so boots
and gloves on, no distractions or deviations;
the Charity Shops can manage without me.

One inch of snow on the beach, two or three
on the roads and railway, and everything stops.
Of course they manage in Norway or Canada,
their medal tally in the Winter Olympics gleams.

Don't get me started on curling, but I do enjoy
ice hockey, my favourite martial arts discipline,
and I have a friend who was a snowboarder
in a previous life; still the bravest woman I know.

She still has that snowboard in her garage,
and if the voice in her head said 'Hey, let's . . .'
she's still got the moves, is stronger than ever,
just in different ways, thinks *Not today.*

Like me, she loved watching those strong women
on the piste, they make her glad she is their Sister,
maybe if no buses are running, we can walk or ski,
meet, share winter weather tales in a warm pub.

MY HEROINE
(after Alexander Samokhvalov, *Girl in a Football Shirt*, 1932)

Now she's my sort of Soviet heroine,
sport is a sort of work; swimmers, soccer
and tennis players lift my heart every time;
strong and sporting women get my vote.

Don't get me wrong, Comrade, I bear
utmost respect for our Sisters in factories,
down the mines, on the Collective Farms,
Heroines of the Revolution every one.

So tell me about the shirt she wears,
I've seen them red, blue, white, pink;
what do these badger stripes represent?
Oh, a gift from an English engineer.

Notts County or Newcastle? These are
coal mining areas, no? True workers
then, Comrade Stalin would approve.
I hope the women there play football.

This one, with her very modern haircut,
reminds me of girl I met when I was 18.
My grandma took me aside and whispered
'She plays for other team, cousin is nice.'

Cousin slapped my face when I spoke of it,
warned about gossip, took me to a poetry
salon, let me be her friend. My admiration
for sporting women is sincere and pure.

A VISION IN PINK
(after Fragonard, *The Swing*, 1767)

I shall send this foolish young man to
catch my shoe presently, I have played
this game before, so has my manservant.
Do you think I would be in Derbyshire
if I did not have my strategy planned?
I am indeed his English rose, approved
by his Papa & Aunts; if he thinks he is
the one catching me or anything of mine,
he is mistaken. Even the stone statues
looking on know better than that.

See how the light shines down on me,
this swing is a marvel of engineering,
could be used as a catapult to ruin castles.
I shall ruin this young gentleman's heart
before I am done, as I think his Mama knows
very well. But I know my duty to my family,
and I shall perform admirably, our children
shall be prodigies; I have hidden talents,
as well as the singing, dancing, playing
the spinet, and household management.

I shall bring my own retinue, my father
has already conferred with the architect
and landscape artist. I am *au courant*
with recent Continental styles and tastes,
my brother made the Grand Tour last year,
my plans shall unfold over time, so that
his Aunts can have no cause to object.
Now, my trusted cousin should be in
position to catch my shoe, we shall see
what this young man has about him.

ONCE UPON A TIME IN JAPAN

There were three bears. They were not real
bears, but bad men transformed for their sins.

Exiled from Edo, they were *ronin*, outlaws.
No homes, no clan, no family, no friends,

not even each other, no women in their lives
out in the wilderness. They did not starve,

every few weeks samurai would seek them out,
pay them to do their Lord's dirty work, things

for which no samurai would risk their honour.
They hid more secrets than a geisha's kimono.

They killed, burned houses with people inside,
stole horses and cattle, abducted children.

Twice a year they moved to a new hideout,
changed their clothes, adopted new accents.

Twenty years of this turned them reckless;
'We need one last reward, then buy an inn.'

They crept into a Matsudaira clan wedding,
took the bride for ransom, who died of shame.

They fled to Hokkaido, a Deva looked down,
decreed *You are beasts, now live as beasts.*

One day they ate the wrong man's sheep,
were hunted, now their heads adorn his hall.

LORD OF CROWS

Welcome to Matsumoto Castle.
It is oldest in Japan, never taken,
never burned or broken. Crow,
they call us, never to our face.

Yet this castle's black wings protect
them from samurai, and outlaws
like your Wild West, except train
that brought you is never robbed.

Have you read Bashō, who tells
of narrow road to deep north?
I sent my second son there,
he returned with tale beyond price.

Oh, he brought gifts, and dowry
for a great wedding, but real prize
was what he told me: *a waterfall
chanting its way down the mountain.*

I want to go there while I still can,
I will leave Elder Son in charge,
return in time for Younger Son's
wedding to his northern blossom.

I am Lord of Crows still, our black
wings strong, I am strong enough
for expedition north, let my sons
meditate that, why we hold title.

TAKE ME TO THE BRIDGE

A garden or a river with a bridge
is always beautiful, no matter what,
we should all have an ideal bridge,
especially if we live in a desert.

A bridge Monet could have painted
and perhaps did, if this is his garden
in Giverny, or an ornamental bridge
in Kyoto, made famous by Hokusai.

One end is closed off; perhaps this
bridge was never meant to be walked
over, or some outcome of unrequited love
happened here under the moonlight.

Is this bridge a monument to love,
and the trees whisper the woman's name
and her ghost re-appears once a month
or once a year and she stands waiting.

Or Monet was right, a bridge is just
a bridge, and has no more meaning
than any other arrangement of lines,
planes & mass, never to be walked on.

Never to be leapt from or rowed under,
its reflection in the water reminding
carp in the pond, passing butterflies,
or people that this is all an illusion.

I AM YOUR BRIDGE

I was here before you, will be here
after you are gone. You talk of yourself
as the custodian of this garden.

You talk too much, humans always talk
too much; the Buddha said 'How rare
to be born a human being.' Thanks be

for that. You imagine that you *touch*
the beauty of the park by the bridge.
You are talking about me, but betray

your own egotism; you do not make
my home beautiful by thinking it so.
You do not make me beautiful either.

Do the effects I produce in your mind
make you want to play your flute and dance?
Or do you want to sit and meditate?

What's the difference between dancing
meditation and sitting meditation?
Shall I show you how to dance?

Google the handbook on building wooden
bridges, in Japanese or American English,
let me know if you understand either.

Everyone always has a different style
The effects of this bridge are very dance
You can wear the same piece of wood

I forget who danced these words into life,
perhaps they came here, alone or with a friend,
carried new words home in their heart.

ONE MORE CUP OF COFFEE
(after Sally Meakins, *I was Thinking of You*)

Yes, that Bob Dylan song, a clock for what
I have to do, down in the valley, it can't wait,

I am not putting it off, I have eaten the apple,
left the evidence, and I don't care who knows.

Always thinking of you, even on the mountain,
I hear the mermaids singing and I answer them,

say I will be in the City again in the Autumn,
will see them at the surfers beach at dawn,

assure them I am never far from the sea,
I dream the tides, even out in the desert

where the sea is the desert's doppelgänger,
or on mountains where rainforest monkeys live.

I see my previous life in this coffee cup,
feel the seeds of my new life in this apple,

will find a good spot to plant these seeds,
a gift for whoever lives, visits, or passes by.

In this cowboy town where nobody knows me,
I will find another coffee shop, log on, start work.

I will drive from town to town, coffee shop
to coffee shop, I don't need a gun, or a pen,

I am your online assassin, can ruin your life
so many ways, I am Kali, virus and viral.

CONFESSION
(after Raphael, *Pope Julius II,* 1511–12)

I believe I need to go to Confession,
I have heard too much, am always
weighed down by sin and wrongdoing.

I know I am Il Papa, Vicar of Christ,
Supreme Pontiff, and infallible,
but still, what I learned this morning,

never mind what happened last night,
causes me to reflect, brings me pain,
but I remain the Warrior Pope still.

I shall summon Sister Mary Stigmata
to hear my confession, beg her to wash away
my sins with her tears, rub my aching back.

I will ask her what she has heard about
what my College of Cardinals is planning,
who among them is still my loyal friend.

I shall find time to listen to the younger
Cardinals, and judge their ambitions,
estimate who among them is pure of heart.

Should I promote them, exile them, or
find them a Province suited to their talents?
And what of my most senior Counsellors?

Is it time to consider their retirement?
I should know which have resources,
a villa in the hills, are one step ahead.

Perhaps I should trust in God's mercy,
prepare my own villa, or keep them
guessing what sort of Father I really am.

OUT FOR A WALK
(after Izis *Île St. Louis, Paris, 1946*)

It is only a year, but feels like forever,
or yesterday, depending on what you did
in the War; this man and woman walking
towards each other, are they strangers

out for a stroll this Autumn morning,
about to pass each other in silence
or will they recognise each other,
say 'Bonjour', arrange to meet later?

Perhaps they know what the other did,
good or bad, maybe share a secret
they will take with them everywhere
and tell to no-one, that ruined lives.

Has the woman's hair grown back,
is the man maimed from a Gestapo
interview, or are they lucky heroes
who refused medals and recognition?

If their lives are full of memories
discarded like the leaves underfoot,
who will blame them, who will ask
after them if they move to the suburbs?

Who can say what is normal now,
or walk down the street, or past
a building without remembering
what might have been done there?

THE VIEW FROM THE VILLA DELIRIUM

Was it really 1973 we were lost in Tangier,
on a flat roof at midnight, early December,
not Kerouac's Villa Munira, but our very own
Villa Delirium, full of posh expats, Vietnam
draft dodgers, smugglers, trust fund novelists,
people we knew better than to even look at.

A full moon backdrop to someone's radio
or record player, or a hidden presence playing live,
the soprano sax's Berber wail our soundtrack,
plates of fish tagine, bottles of Casablanca beer
to hand, what might have been a piano somewhere,
or just in my head, my heart miming a bass guitar.

Realising very slowly that we had lost the moon,
the night was no longer dark, a shifting curtain
falling over us, and yes, it was snowing in Tangier,
not just over our lone rooftop, but everywhere,
a special gift, even though we had seen and felt
snow, but especially for children of all ages here,

who had maybe seen snow on TV but not for real,
had never felt really cold air in their lungs or on
the face, never scooped up a handful of fresh snow
or tried to dance on it, and all too soon we went
indoors and slept through the rest of this change,
and woke to a city of wonder, children's laughter,

adults shrugging 'Inshallah', *God's Will* the answer
to whatever question. Back then we had no camera
or iDevice, but I promise you this really happened,
as if Tangier had been translated to the Atlas Mountains,
or the mountains had come to Tangier, whatever god
you might believe in, just testing to see who is awake.

MAKING NEW MUSIC
Play What You Don't Know (Miles Davis)

To know the changes, then realise
you don't need to know the changes,

to play modal, and not worry about 'right',
or Buddy Bolden or Louis Armstrong,

however brave they were in their day,
this is your time, you have been called,

 don't look around, don't turn aside,
or think about what Bird or Trane did,

let yourself squawk or squeal, just keep
going, trust yourself, trust the drummer,

know that you are all leaders on this
stand today, you are nobody's sideman,

your audience is with you all the way,
 will come with you, next step and beyond,

 will say to their kids in years to come,
I was there, for them as much as you,

this is only the start of this journey,
one step, a thousand miles, out into

interstellar space, you are all together,
every note an invitation to love,

where what you don't know
is what you knew all along.

INTERVIEW: MY EARLY MEMORIES

I recall patchwork fields, green then gold,
but almost nothing else; I was four years old
and barely remember the man with the thick
black moustache they said was my father.

Of course I remember my mother, grandmother,
the two girls who might have been my sisters,
all dressed the same, in long black dresses, boots,
and blue headscarves, but not my brothers.

They went away, and never came back,
so many men who never came back,
some who wrote letters or sent parcels,
two or three times a year, some who did not.

So I grew up in a house of women,
like most of the other boys in our townland,
and if ever I missed out on anything, who
was to know, all our lives were the same.

Three days after my grandmother died,
two men with hard hats and harder faces
handed my mother a sheaf of papers; that was
the day I learned our family owned nothing.

A train, a town, a factory, a school, all new,
so much *strange* at once, I will not repeat
the words we were called, only now know
how my mother saved 10 years to get us here.

Were those green and gold fields really ours?
I do not know, any more than I can speak
my grandmother's tongue, but when I play
the music you think so new, she sings through me.

TED HUGHES' FOX

Might have been a real fox once,
Ted writing it while Sylvia slept,
maybe an urban fox in Cambridge,
or one local to Heptonstall's fields,

but the fox, or its shadow is lame,
has been caught in a trap or shot,
and may not survive till morning,
may not make it back to its den.

Its cubs might go hungry, might
be trapped themselves, or fed to
the hounds, their blood smeared
on youthful faces one morning.

Or they might live another day,
then another, reach Summer strong,
make their own lives till their luck
traps them in the wrong field.

This fox has written part of its own
life into the snow's blank page,
to be read or ignored by the rest
of its world, one story of many.

How can we or this fox know
each other, read each other's lives,
understand each other's hearts,
or share a common midnight?

ZORRO

It will be fifteen years or so before the boy
in this caravan site photo learns any Spanish,
won't get much further than 'Otra cerveza
por favor' in Torremolinos and Barcelona.

On this August day he does not know 'zorro'
means fox in Spanish, enjoys the TV show
or Saturday cinema in Glasgow for the action,
the dashing man in black outwitting enemies.

He does not know the California he will grow
to love in the Sixties was still part of New
Spain, before Mexico won independence,
that some people might call Zorro a terrorist.

He has a plastic sword, rides a red bicycle,
has never heard the word 'vigilante',
perhaps compares Zorro to Robin Hood,
and knows who has right on their side.

There are no Irish Rebel songs sung or played
in his or his grandparents' house, he has seen
Orange Order parades, knew better than to go
home and ask *Daddy, what's a fenian barsteward?*

And now he is a long way from Glasgow,
says to anyone who asks would he return,
'The climate would kill me'; some things
don't change, even if the darkest days are past.

HIS FINAL JOURNEY
(i.m. Gerry Docherty, 3/4/1935 - 4/3/2018)

The hardest part wasn't launching the longship,
Amazon shipped that same day from Bergen,

a better service than Harrods or Neiman Marcus,
the black sail was a strong rune, the fibreglass model

steersman looked quite realistic; bystanders asked
if we were making a film and could they be extras,

I recited 'the boy stood on the burning deck/whence all
but he had fled' and they slunk away, but most of them

had the wrong tattoos, like the extras who auditioned for
Braveheart to be told nobody had King Billy tats in 1297.

Getting the boat properly ablaze took a few bales of straw
and a barrel of chip shop oil from the Baltic Fish Bar.

By the time he reached Clydebank the sail was sending up
a good gold flame that looked great on the Six O'Clock News,

and burned till the cameras lost interest, and beyond;
we followed in the motor launch borrowed for the day.

The challenge was navigating the Clyde's hidden currents,
but Dad's old mates from Rolls Royce custom built a 100hp

engine with remote control, that could have powered an
early biplane; did they use genuine Rolls Royce spares?

The weather was perfect as he faded into the western light,
we reached The Gantocks, raised a glass of Glenmorangie

to 'Big Gerry' while 'I Left My Heart in San Francisco' played
and cheered; 'Aye, on his way to Valhalla, right enough.'

ON BEING TAKEN FOR A MING VASE

Suddenly I am old, precious, and fragile.
Well, I know that anyway, but it's good
that someone else recognises this fact.

I'm used to giving up my seat on the Tube
for older people, pregnant women, or just
anyone I like the look of; my turn now.

Yes, this is happening for me, young people,
men or women, are offering me their seat,
Oh, do you mean me? Do I look fragile,

*am I channelling your Grandad, or Funny
Uncle? Flattered I am,* to paraphrase Yoda,
I don't look like him yet, but I am not ready

to be invisible as a person, or seen as a
Harmless Old Man, who might collapse
in a heap, if not at the very least, offered

a seat, I should appreciate this courtesy
while it lasts, not say *Look, I still have
something to offer, I am still young inside,*

*I know things you don't, have done things
you haven't, seen things and been places,
can amuse you, or show you a good time,*

*but won't, am on my way to visit my special
friend, we are not yet* Old and in The Way,
we will enjoy our day, might outlive you.

But I will take your seat, I have a good way
to go, but remember this; all that matters
is Love, in all its glory, and all its forms.

THE BLUEST FLOWER
Pick a flower on Earth and you move the farthest star. (Paul Dirac)

That was how the Gaia Hypothesis was explained
by a Star Pilot from Proxima B who crashed
near Roswell and lived to tell his tale to me.

He thought he was talking about the mathematics
of gravity, but after a few beers and two burgers
I knew better, then the band started playing,

but by the time they played the 'Tennessee Waltz'
he was weeping into his beer and turning it blue.
Well, the cowboys just watched us for a while

then turned away, but not before one muttered
'Suppose they'll be doing a shadow dance next.'
When the singer announced 'He'll Have To Go'

we took the hint and climbed into his shuttle craft
which mimed a 57 Cadillac Eldorado perfectly,
and rolled sedately past the Highway Patrol.

'Don't worry, my cousin works for them, he was
an extra in *Men In Black*, I can talk the talk.'
I nearly said 'Yeah, but can you walk the walk?'

He wept again when we drove up to my uncle's
cabin, and saw the prettiest field of blue flowers.
Blue and bluer, we talked a blue streak till sunup.

Then we sang Hank Williams' 'I Saw the Light'
and swore we were friends for life after learning
both of our wives are buried under blue meadows.

He drove to Taos, where spare parts are disguised
as trash art, his last words 'A blue star in your dreams
signals *I hope there's some cold beer in your fridge.*'

COMPATIBLE

If the car chooses the driver,
who knows where they will go,

or how far on their road together,
and if the radio repeats 'Route 66'

the driver should take the hint
and ask which she would prefer,

Interstate 40 or the Mother Road,
or switch when the going gets rough.

So, Chicago to Santa Monica,
could be your best two weeks ever,

or more if you make new friends
or pick up the right hitchhikers.

If she says, the first time you meet,
'Hello, my name is Christine',

what could possibly go wrong?
Real life is not a Stephen King novel.

Maybe you'd better not miss out
any of the places named in the song,

and not even think about New Orleans
if you don't like Oklahoma and fancy

a detour, just observe the speed limit
through New Mexico and Arizona,

as for Las Vegas, not on this map,
that's another trip for another year.

CROSSROADS

Like Robert Johnson, I am *standing*
at the crossroads, I don't think I sold
my soul for guitar mastery; who knows
what I or my doppelgänger just did,

and what the aftershock might be,
my debts for seven years, a lifetime,
or eternity; for this day, a good band,
decent food, and some loving please.

It's not yet dawn, not even grey yet,
who knows what traffic might flow
through from any of these roads,
or if I might get run over by rednecks.

I am frozen to this spot, but won't risk
those dark fields' unknown hazards;
if I accept a lift, who takes me where,
or maybe my journey ends in a ditch.

Soon, the sun will tell me East from West,
show me a choice, which road to follow
into a town that I hope is friendly, a train
or Greyhound bus to take me Somewhere.

Don't say *hope is for fools*, or *my heart*
will show me the right road to follow,
but if a 57 Cadillac Eldorado slows down
for me, I will climb in gladly and sit back.

PHOENIX FINDS HAPPINESS

It's our new home in California,
just along the road from Eureka.

This is a haven for rich old hippies
who escaped from Haight-Ashbury

before hard drugs contaminated
the counter-culture; they sold up,

cleaned up, meditate twice a day
and are so smug and self-centred.

My best friend and I just bought
one of the only two bars in town.

We will be flying the Rainbow Flag,
out and proud, making a difference

in Happiness, California, our aim
is *Think global, dance local,*

and anyone who doesn't like it
can drink in the Glockamorra Bar

at the other end of Main Street;
tolerance goes about 200 yards here.

We welcome anyone who welcomes us,
and yes, we will show football on TV.

Oh yeah, we will be running for Sheriff
and Mayor, is that your worst nightmare?

ON A CLEAR DAY
(after Maureen Gallace, *Sandy Road*, 2003)

This is not a road, it is a destination.
Nobody knows, not even us or the IRS,
how we got here, what we did to get here.

Is this an endless highway, or a coda to
the Golden Road to Unlimited Devotion?
You tell me & if I believe you, I'll marry you.

Oh, you're not . . . not what? I don't care if you're
Other, Whatever, we are all Resident Aliens here,
why do you think the houses here lie at odd angles?

Did you notice a white picket fence anywhere?
Don't be shy, you'll get to know us all real soon,
appreciate our quirks, learn *Love Thy Neighbour*.

Oh, we used up all those Bibles years ago,
and any other reading material we could find,
it's all good, all goes into our daily exchanges.

We talk with each other all the time, on the porch,
in the Supermarket, after dinner, we have a radio
station, but we have no TV or radio out here.

Oh sure, laptops, tablet, they're not illegal,
neither are most other things you can persuade
to work, and someone might have spares.

If you join us, bring some stuff we might need,
or haven't seen in a while, be ready to barter,
and learn to love having folks round for meals.

So, are we friends forever? I truly hope so,
these mountains behind you are 40 miles away,
first snowfall might be sooner than you think.

UNDER A BLUE SKY

That is how I normally live in Colorado,
how I want to live, under the sun or snow,
the mountains backstopping everything I do.

So when people told me England is grey,
London has no sky, then said 'Why would
you want to go there?' I replied, 'Friends.'

'But you have friends here, what's wrong
with us, no need to go anywhere else.'
They're right, I would die without friends.

My friends are scattered but never lost,
I do Six Degrees of Separation really well,
so I travel, they travel, all roads are one.

Now, in Richmond, the sky is grey, the Thames
is grey, it must have rained in the early hours,
but there is a thin wash of blue to the west.

In my west, my true west, only seven hours
behind, dawn has woken people, dogs and deer,
and snow is sliding down the mountains.

Not avalanche, just another quiet morning
in the Sangre de Cristo Mountains, soon
the cyclists will fuel up for training runs.

And everyone in Westcliffe, all 600 of them,
will go about their daily business, quietly,
without fuss, no hurry, no worry about anything.

My friends will show me Richmond Park, Hampton
Court Palace, and tomorrow, Kew Gardens, but this
grey sky is what I will remember on the plane home.

PROVINCETOWN, 1951
(after Edward Hopper, *Rooms By The Sea*)

The light has been moving around this room
and this house for hours; I did not salute
the sunrise or watch the fishermen setting
out for their day's work in the earliest hours,
and they might have returned safely while
I was eating breakfast, or reading the paper.

Their catch, good or bad, gone to market,
and maybe by now, in a restaurant or hotel
kitchen in Manhattan, being turned into art,
or a simple traditional dish from a secret
recipe the chef swears he learned from his
Nonna who was born in the old country.

Or maybe I am the only person in town
who does not know that a boat foundered,
a man was washed overboard, or the shoals
of cod they set out to win eluded them.
If I go into town for a bowl of chowder
the room could fall silent as I enter.

The answer to any question is always
in the light, under the sun or the Pole Star,
every day I take whatever light is available,
let it use me for its own purposes, and if
anyone wants to know what I do all day,
that is the best answer I could offer them.

JUNKYARD SQUIRREL
(after Pål Hermansen, *Bumper Life*)

I am living in the mouth of a giant turtle.
It has been out of its native water longer
than I can count, but it gets rained on often.

I do not know its name, call him Mr. Volvo,
or where he came from, but he is my home,
my refuge and my larder; call me Mr. Lucky.

Why am I not living in a forest or garden?
Perhaps I have more than one home, most
Swedes have two, those who can, go South.

Just look at those eyes, they scare off cats,
and confuse stray dogs and reindeer, but
there are no bears in this neighbourhood.

So I am safe and warm, barely notice Winter.
Autumn is my busiest season, gathering food
and bedding for my den, patrolling my territory.

I am always alert, always on the move,
this place keeps me fat, sleek and strong,
I like to chase cats, just to wake them up.

Soon, it will snow again, but I am ready,
enough food hidden, have earned my rest,
will sleep my time away with one eye open.

Perhaps I was a wizard in a previous life,
why this place has been off the man map,
till they customise this part of my world.

STEPPING INTO AUTUMN AT 65

A time of new beginnings, a time for journeys,
a chance to meet new people, discover new places,

store up memories to get me through Winter.
I have just returned again from San Francisco,

and know that I can never live there now,
even for say, seven years, because I am afraid

as I have never been before, after seeing my father
lose weight and muscle tone, so that a short walk

to the pub was almost too much, then Alzheimer's
kicked in hard and sudden; this biggest and strongest

of men became a shadow who had to ask my Mum
'Who was that guy with the beard who was here?'

and who asked me on the phone, 'How's Rose?'
forgetting that she is gone, and I do not want

to toboggan down that slope into darkness;
when my GP asks me about our family history,

I remember that my Nana went that way; I wonder
how long my Autumn will last, where I will spend

the last stage of this journey, and whether it will
matter, if I know anyone there or then, and whether

anyone will know me; in the meantime, this moment
is all there is, and the weather is surprisingly good.

FOR THE FIRST TIME IN MY LIFE

I have a favourite taqueria, named for local hero
Pancho Villa, on 16th Street in San Francisco.

I was not disappointed by anything I found here,
by the panoramic mural of Villa on the outside wall,

the bust of Villa blessing the food above the kitchen,
the painting of Pancho galloping into history at Zacateca,

and certainly not by the freshly made Mission-style burritos,
guachinango tacos & enchiladas enjoyed on successive days,

and I am sure I can hear different flavours of Spanish
around me as I eat, and among the cooking crew,

but there are also a few Anglos here, not tourists
like me, but local hipsters, we are all welcome,

the same good food and aguas frescas offered to all,
this is The City, not Donald Trump's America,

he might close this place if he ever heard about it,
and build a wall round The Mission District.

I would like to bring my compañera Alice here for lunch
before we walk under The Castro's Rainbow flags,

we can have our burritos or tacos exactly how we desire,
with fish, *sin carne*, spicy sauce or mild, and just enjoy,

no longer tourists, but guests, so much to explore,
and Alice can start to know and love the City as I do.

DARK WAS THE NIGHT

(after Andrew Harston, *Bottle Alley*, 2017)

And cold is the ground every time
in Homeless Town; not by your choice,
maybe not even by parents, bosses,
or landlords choice, but just because . . .

Once you're out in the darkness,
where the stars do not shine for you,
and there is never a scent of jasmine
or bougainvillea, that darkness claims you.

You will carry it in your heart,
walk in a cloud of darkness wherever
you go; if you are lucky you will be
known and accepted by your new peers.

Maybe Golden Gate Park's homeless colony
will say 'Hey, Brother, sit with us awhile'
or Market St. will give you a new name
and say 'That used to be Tom's doorway.'

On the #6 bus from Market to Haight,
you will listen to a tourist tell his new
friend about the climate in Hastings
or Glasgow: *Oh man, that sounds mean.*

That place, Bottle Alley, is too familiar,
you know how things could end there,
anyone putting coin in your cup goes home,
won't give a little more tax to save your life.

A RIPPLE WIDENING

It can be anything, anywhere,
an echo from a round flat stone
skimmed across Hermit Lake
in Colorado, by a friend there,

or a different stone skipping across
a pond in Alexandra Park by a boy
trying to impress his pals, or done
casually, precisely, on his own

or a silent echo in a Zen temple
in Kyoto, an unintended slip
of the rake, that the head monk
will order re-done, or might let be,

or a ripple in the mind on hearing
a favourite song, or seeing someone
smile, or someone in the sunlit Park
recalling a day spent with a friend,

the echoes within us and without us
move out or stay within, to be
released one day on the mountain
or another day hearing live jazz.

No point worrying where they go,
if they merge or harmonise with other
echoes, and if we touch others or
others touch us, then be grateful.

POSSIBILITIES
Anything can happen in the next half-hour ('Stingray' TV series)

Half an hour could be an eternity
even for the walking talking puppets

in *Team America*'s adult version
of *Thunderbirds*, and who knows

what their unscripted downtime
involves in Beverly Hills or Malibu,

even for us, half an hour could be
the rest of our lives, so at our wake,

whatever we've seen or did is backstory
for our friends & family to talk about,

remember or forget, and whether there is
a light or *out go the lights,* we can only hope

we did our best on any given day
and maybe if there was a bright day

we were given a glimpse of a possibility,
let that be our last memory, and hope

it might happen, so if we had a dream
where an absent friend or the love

of our life came through the turnstile,
exactly as we choose to remember them,

then whatever we imagine 'reality' is,
could happen, could transmute,

could take us somewhere we have
not allowed ourselves to dream of.

POTENTIAL

Most new-born sentient creatures
know nothing, apart from hunger.

How lucky, you say, of the alligator hatchling
which opens its hungry eye and swims off

and catches a frog five seconds later,
and the gleam of triumph in its little eye

is truly terrifying, because we know
that tiny fragile creature will grow

and its hunger will grow with it,
and grow it, and that hunger is

all there is to it, it needs nothing else,
perfect and perfected, exactly as is,

that alligator knows with certainty
its place in the world, something we

have to learn, by ourselves, from parents,
or whoever will tutor or nurture us,

but we learn soon enough that we have
potential, that we are works in progress,

and who knows what our boundaries are,
and if there is a sin in the world, it is

that our wings are clipped, that some
of us might never be able to fly free.

SO YOU THINK

That I am an ostrich and that is all I am;
foolishness, what you think you know about me

is not true, I have never stuck my head in the sand
as if that would make me invisible and invulnerable.

I am stronger than you, can break your bones
and leave you for the hyenas, if you get too close.

As for flying, I can do that better than you,
I need no artificial aids to go where I please.

Even now, I am soaring above you,
can fly to the moon and back, or round

the world in a heartbeat; can you do that now?
I can visit my cousins down under whenever

I choose, or they can come here, we could even
be in both places at once if we choose, and

you would never know; you think you know
everything and own everything, but you know

nothing, you own nothing, have failed to be
the good steward you were brought here for.

If I ask if you understand the difference between
'looking' and 'seeing', what's your answer?

One last thing: if you have a heart,
look into it, that's all, that's really all.

DISTRACTIONS

There are too many of those in the world.
Not just things, or music, art or movies.

It is not enough to turn the TV off,
or put our laptops or phones away,

or stop buying newspapers or magazines,
as if not paying attention to events is enough.

If the world changes around us,
and we have not noticed or are indifferent,

what good is that? If you are looking
for Enlightenment, where will you find it?

If I had that answer, I would ask you
to buy my book that will tell you how,

but maybe that book, if I have written it,
and not been distracted by *Poirot* repeats,

is just another distraction, just a few more
words to add to the mind's chatter.

If I said *All you need is a pure heart
and an empty mind*, would you believe me?

If I said *All you need is Love,* or *All you need
is cash*, could you believe both or neither?

To be present in the Now, but remember
to pay the utility bills, is that a paradox?

To love someone wholeheartedly, but
let them go their own way, can you do that?

IF WE HAVE OUR OWN MYTH

How do we discover it;
do we join a meditation group,
practice yoga, join our local Sangha,

or go off into the desert
or up the mountain again,
or try to do something memorable

so that others, whether friends
or enemies, will create that myth
for us, how we will be remembered.

Or will we look into our heart
and examine every memory
we can stand, as if we have

walked into a carpet shop
and stood patiently while
the owner unfolds every carpet

or rug till we find one that
is right for us, that we can
live with, that can live with us,

and be with us everywhere
we go, so that even people
who never met us before

will say *This is a man I want
to get to know*, and we will
let them get to know us,

so that we enact our myth,
and it becomes its own truth,
and that is who we are.

HOLY DOG

For bringing us the horse, we could almost forgive you
for bring us whiskey. Horses make a landscape look
more beautiful. (Lame Deer, Lakota Seeker of Visions)

When the Lakota looked on the horses
the Conquistadors brought to Turtle Island
they called them Holy Dog, no doubt
recalling *Eohippus*, who stood knee-high.

Now, horses are lost from most landscapes,
people drive pickups and drink whiskey,
preferably never at the same time,
or in the wrong order, or drink alone.

Friends make a landscape more beautiful
as we pass through, stay a while, dance,
share a glass; may we all meet our Holy Dog,
sacred companion to guide us on our way.

YULETIDE 2018

LETTING GO

Some mornings I feel that my house
is an unmoored narrowboat and I am

moving slowly but steadily downriver
and soon I will reach the tidal stretch

and before I know it, perhaps even
before breakfast, I will be headed out

to sea, and into the shipping lanes
where if I am lucky, I will end up

in Holland or Brittany and I will eat
brunch in Dutch or Breton, then go

to meet the local mermaids, who might
give me a conch shell all the way from

the Caribbean, and tell me to listen
to the voices within, every morning

and last thing at night, and if this happens,
yes I will listen, and believe what I hear,

becoming one with the flow, because I know
that the voices will never lie to me.

BLUE FEBRUARY

Today is a blue day,
not because I am blue
but because we are past
midwinter, away from
black mornings, beyond
grey and now things could
go green or stay blue,
a sky blue, or midnight
blue, and maybe I am
seeing the world like
a cat or sheep, not much
red or orange in my
spectrum, and I am
walking into the light
and who knows what
I might see one day,
and it could be time
to re-learn the difference
between looking & seeing,
today it is time to walk
down to the far end
of Rock-a-Nore, and listen
to the mermaids again,
I have been indoors
too much, I need some
fresh air, and a word
from them in my ear.

SEEING, REALLY SEEING

Every day I look at the sea,
through my window, a bus
or train going to Brighton,
or walking the shore in whatever
weather, and I have realised
that this phenomenon I saw
as grey or blue or green has
a varieties of shadings that must
drive painters mad, or give them
ideas that they will understand
everything if they manage to
represent one moment of the
sea's life almost successfully.
But I knew this anyway, even
when I was half-blinded by
cataracts, and now that I have
good eyesight for the first
time, I do not care if I see
accurately, I am just grateful
that I see truly for the first time,
and I am meditating holidays
in places where their sea & sky
have colours so exotic we think
the local artists have hallucinated
them, or that they should abandon
acrylic paints and go back to
grinding pigments and making
their own unique paints by hand
so that we can believe we could
live by their sea under their sky.

GUIDING STAR

Yet another sleepless night, and you
looked out on the Pole Star's silver
wheel, for once you were not afraid
of the dark, or bothered by the cold,
and you thought of the blood-red
Wolf Moon that you had not stayed
up late enough to see for yourself,
but now you wondered if that moon
could be your new guiding star,
never replacing the Pole Star,
or perhaps only on nights like this,
but the idea of this unique moon
that only you or like-minded people
could hold in your heart, would
warm you on the darkest day,
and you could keep moving forward,
not even with any goal or aim
in mind, and even if you were
just sitting in your chair looking
out to sea or watching TV, *no need
to do anything* your mantra for today,
you have food in the fridge, your home
is warm, you have friends to meet
later or tomorrow, when so many
people have none of these things,
so maybe the days you feel trapped
in your home or stranded in this town,
will be over soon, and you might be
ready to let whichever guiding star
shines for you, guide you on a new path.

MAN IN THE MOON

He has been up there a long time,
ever since his birthplace, Earth 2,
imploded and, among other things,
created our Moon out of the debris.

He thinks of it as his Forever Home,
so was glad the visitors did not do any
lasting damage, but upset that they did
not ask permission to take souvenirs.

Unlike hotels or bars, he cannot order
extra towels or glasses and write it off
as expenses, but he hopes the astronauts
learned something from their trip.

He was saddened they were all men,
he is not human as we live this word,
so wanted to meet a spacewoman,
just talk to her, and brighten his day.

If there might be a Woman in the Moon,
he has not met her, he hasn't lost hope,
and wishes one day a passing starship
will send a landing party to stay a while.

And yet even if he lives on the dark side,
maybe he has two hearts, is lit from within,
has visited our dreams, with gifts, and we
can return the favour when we are ready.

WEST OF IRELAND LIGHT
(after Graham Crowley, *Yellow Rockery*, 2003)

Today, everything is golden, even the roof
and all the window frames of this house.

How this happened, no-one knows,
and since it is not even noon, cannot

say how the rest of the day will turn out.
As for tomorrow, even thinking that far

ahead would be asking for trouble,
so today, everyone will close the shutters

and stay at home, perhaps not even go
to the pub and discuss this three beer

problem; if anyone is praying for guidance
they will keep that to themselves, it could

be a sign, a warning, or the aftermath
of some event they do not yet know about.

Or maybe two people have fallen in love
and this is the gold of their hearts overflowing

and because everything is right with their world,
everyone around can share their good fortune.

THERE IS ALWAYS HOPE
(after Banksy, *Girl With Balloon*)

And there is always a red balloon,
in the hand or heart of a child,
perhaps old enough to understand
what she is about to do, or maybe
this is a rehearsal for what comes
next, when she will have to give
her heart away, whether or not
she is ready, let us hope whoever
is offered her heart accepts gratefully
and is good to her, and is worthy
of this gift, but if not, they will
both learn from this, and however
much it hurts, will be willing
to try again, and not hold back
or turn aside, and they can look
up at the stars and hold up
their balloon to the winds of
the world, and stand where they are,
or walk on till they meet the right
Someone who also holds up their
balloon, and they look into each
other's eyes, and know that they
hold one balloon together, that
their song will always be Bob Marley's
'One Love', and that they will
indeed enjoy perfect unity.

MONKEY BRIDGE

You can find them in most parts of the world,
what we in *El Norte* call the Third World,
Latin America, India, Nepal, any space
too small for Western Engineering, but
just the right size for local ingenuity.

And perhaps we are all monkeys
in the eyes of whatever God or No-God
you might believe in, and you will
need faith, luck, and local knowledge
to cross the bridge and stroll on.

If you have to cross this bridge to reach
something or someone, do not hesitate
or someone else might eat your lunch
or steal your luck, or meet the person
who could have been the love of your life.

There is always a bridge, swaying gently
or creaking loudly, sometimes the bridge
might not be ready for you to cross it,
you could meet the other cliff face first
or plunge down into the torrent below.

But only you can know if you are ready,
or how fast you can dance across those
planks or rope, but if your steps are light
and your heart is true, maybe the bridge
will allow you to be lucky one more time.

DUCHESS, BORDERLESS
(after Clara Kleine, *The Woman*)

I am your Duchess Toomuchness,
I have more to offer than you can

imagine, I am not illegal,
I am not immoral, I am beyond

these notions, and beyond
your dreams; I am not stateless

but I have no country, walls
cannot contain me, you cannot

exclude me or imprison me,
I am the future you fear,

I am the past you ignore
and despise, to your cost.

You cannot imagine what
I am capable of, and so

you think the worst of me,
not the best I could offer;

do I bring out the worst in you,
the darkness from your past?

Oh, Mr President,
do not be afraid of me,

embrace me and I will
make America great again.

FRANK EXPLORES THE FRENCH QUARTER

I found Bourbon Street's *Treasure Isle*,
live Cajun music, cold beer, and a room
full of folks who could waltz and two-step,
and met Heidi who made me feel at home.

The accordionist intro'd a song about a man
who found four reasons not to get married,
'Who's married?' A forest of hands raised,
'Who's thinking of getting married?'

No-one, so I raised my hand; 'Ok, when?'
'Not sure, *ma chérie* is being cautious.'
So I told my new friend Heidi about you,
showed her your photo; 'She's beautiful.'

Heidi was well qualified to judge. On Friday,
someone said 'Where's your lady friend?'
'Gone back to Pennsylvania, but I hope
we'll keep in touch' and I raised my glass.

My special request that night was 'Jolie Blonde',
they sang it in French, but I got the message,
a man's partner leaves him for another man,
but, 'lots more pretty blondes in the world.'

Maybe 'Diggy Liggy Lo' is the only happy
Cajun song, if getting married and having
kids is your idea of happiness, but hey,
chérie, let's do the Cajun dance anyway.

IN THE MOMENT

It sounds as if Dionysus has won
the eternal argument with Apollo.

Just do it is much too simple,
someone has to check the brakes

and gas up your Harley or you won't
be heading down Highway 101,

or maybe might not take that bend,
and you could wake up in ER or

your next life, but yes, there
is a moment you must be in,

just waiting for you to fill it
and move on, into the next one

and the one after, till you meet
your brothers, and accept a cold

beer and a plate of food, some
music to dance to, and a friend

to embrace, and that is now,
and that is eternity, what more

could you ask, and if Dionysus
and Apollo want to step outside,

that's their business, you have
the beer, the food, and the moves.

TRIAD
(after Michael Rothenstein, *Three Women By The Sea*)

Whether they are three Sisters or Three Fates,
or three random women the Artist has invented,
or his regular models, is not important today.

What is important is not your business
and not for the ears of men, and the music
shared by the left-handed guitarist

owes nothing to Picasso, or Wallace Stevens'
'Man with the Blue Guitar'; these women
have no time for surrealist games, they do

indeed playthings as they are, and perhaps
are making a new music that will change
the world; this is 1938 after all, they know

about the coming storm, already their
friends and relatives are being denied
visas, and having their lives confiscated.

So our guitarist plays on, and they sing,
as if making a soundtrack for a movie where
escape to America or Anywhere is possible.

They have eaten lunch, perhaps enjoyed
a glass of wine, but not made plans to meet
again, as if that might be too much to ask.

I WISH, SHE SAID, YOU WERE A GARDENER

My friend the Whenever Gardener
gave me lunch, and shared her dream
of a spontaneous meadow planting,
leaving her formal garden behind;
I wish my dreams were this beautiful,
but I still love to visit formal gardens,
with no responsibilities or duties,

perhaps these gardens were attached to
a Palladian villa, sustained by money
that came from Venice originally, or
were the private part of an estate in
the antebellum South, where the stain
of slavery is almost erased, and visitors
or guests can enjoy walking through
the garden or grounds at minuet speed,

the modern world a few minutes away
but distant till we reach the Gift Shop,
then the carpark, but meantime let
us enjoy the variety of plants, herbs,
and trees living in fellowship today,
who would have been strangers once,
competing for water, minerals, light,

but now, they have no need to do so,
example to us all, but a bygone hand
brought them here, and other hands
maintain the balance and order today,
chance is not accident, weeds need
not be strangers here, the sundial
sends its shadow round the borders,
and never pauses or looks back.

SOFT DAY IN ST. LEONARDS
(after Maureen Harman, *Untitled*)

Today, the sheep are walking on water.
Why they are doing this, or where they
are going, nobody I spoke to knows.

They are fading into the sea-mist quietly,
as if they are walking on the spot,
or forming a chorus line, an audition

for a new production that will re-define
diversity in East Sussex; oh, you didn't
know that sheep have personalities,

and have a range of talents and abilities;
just wait till they start singing & dancing
then you will learn what individuality

can mean today, you will pay to see this,
follow their Arts Council-sponsored Tour
round the country, and possibly become

one of their groupies, if they will accept you
as friend or ally, and you promise to live
vegan, and join your local Buddhist sangha.

Most of them are not human-phobic,
but there are sheep-friendly spaces
where you can be a tolerated tourist.

Get over yourself, accept them for who
they truly are, even when their fleece changes
colour in today's climate, and they own

the rainbow, because they know they are
beautiful, and soon they will move off
in formation, into the bluebell woods.

MERMAID ON THE BEACH

(after Dawn Timmins, *Mermaid on the Beach*)

Don't get me wrong, young man,
I am not sad, not waiting for you
or anyone, am not even missing
my sisters, who will be back soon.

You don't even know who St. Leonard
is, do you? I don't think he ever walked
this beach, maybe never set foot on any
French beach, or left the forest of Limousin.

He is, among other roles, patron saint
of lost causes and pregnant women;
you look like a lost cause to me,
and no, I have never been pregnant.

If you knew anything about me,
you might guess why my hair
is not green today, why my nails
are red, but you are Captain Clueless.

Do you know, I think I will go to
Brighton tomorrow, meet my sisters
there, and we will take part in the
March of the Mermaids, liven it up.

Oh yes, let's redefine magic realism,
and if there are any prizes for best
costume, we will claim those, and
give our human sisters a day to remember.

LOSING SIGHT OF THE SHORE

And the mermaids are waving goodbye.
If they used electronics they would text
or email *Bye for now*, *ciao*, or *sayonara*,
because they know they or their sisters
will see me or someone like me, again.

They never lose sight of their shore,
but lose sight of people all too often,
and think us foolish and hasty in our
little lives, and do not like surprises.
They prefer to live with one horizon.

This was only ever a short-term berth,
I won't look back or think of the people
I drank with last night without telling
them *That was last orders*. In a few weeks,
Captain Clueless will do a Facebook post.

Tomorrow, given a fair wind, and no storms,
I hope to set foot on a new shore dreamt of
for fifty years, stow my gear in the hostel
I am booked into, then find a bar to enjoy
the local wine and music with a new friend.

I will fly the flag of *No Regrets* and not think
of the books, CDs, or anything else jettisoned,
but walk the town until I know where I am,
learn which neighbourhood will suit me,
anchor there, and learn to love my new shore.